Gold Seekers

Life on the Australian Goldfields

Nicolas Brasch

Gold Seekers: Life on the Australian Goldfields

Text: Nicolas Brasch
Publishers: Tania Mazzeo and Eliza Webb
Series consultant: Amanda Sutera
Hands on Heads Consulting
Editor: Gemma Smith
Project editors: Annabel Smith and Jarrah Moore
Designer: Leigh Ashforth
Project designer: Danielle Maccarone
Illustrations: Martin Sanders
Permissions researchers: Catherine Kerstjens and Lumina Datamatics
Production controller: Renee Tome

Acknowledgements
We would like to thank the following for permission to reproduce copyright material:

Front cover: Edward Roper/Dixson Galleries, State Library of New South Wales; pp. 1, 19 (top): American & Australasian Photographic Company/Mitchell Library, State Library of New South Wales pp. 3, 17 (bottom): Atomic/Alamy Stock Photo; p. 4: Egyptian necklace: BOOCYS/Shutterstock.com, Roman coins: iStock.com/Wirestock, Chinese goblet: Purchase, 2001 Benefit Fund, 2002/The Metropolitan Museum of Art, Mayan jewellery: p. 5 (top): INTERFOTO/Alamy Stock Photo, (bottom): iStock.com/xavierarnau; p. 6 (top): Hans/Adobe Stock, (bottom left): iStock.com/Kondor83, (bottom right): Andris Torms/Dreamstime.com; p. 7 (top): Maren Winter/Shutterstock.com, (middle): Dan74/Shutterstock.com, (bottom): UPI/Alamy Stock Photo; p. 10: Balcombe, T. (Thomas), 1810 -1861/Mitchell Library, State Library of New South Wales; p. 11: Angas, George French, 1822-1886 Lacy, George, 1816-1878/State Library of New South Wales; p. 12 (top): Ballarat Heritage Services, (bottom): Prout, John Skinner. (1852). Alluvial gold washing, Mt Alexander goldfields, Victoria, ca. 1852. Retrieved from http://nla.gov.au/nla.obj-137384301; p. 14: Niday Picture Library/Alamy Stock Photo; p. 15 (top): Russell, C. J. W. (1853). Butchers Gulley, Aug. 22, 1853., (bottom): Mitchell Library, State Library of New South Wales; p. 16 (left): KGPA Ltd/Alamy Stock Photo, (top right): BW Folsom/Shutterstock.com, (middle right, p. 32): VTR/Alamy Stock Photo; p. 17 (top): GRANGER - Historical Picture Archive/Alamy Stock Photo; p. 18: American & Australasian Photographic Company/Mitchell Library, State Library of New South Wales; p. 19 (bottom): American & Australasian Photographic Company/Mitchell Library, State Library of New South Wales; p. 20: State Library of Victoria; p. 21 (top): American & Australasian Photographic Company/Mitchell Library, State Library of New South Wales, (bottom): Lakeview Images/Alamy Stock Photo; p. 22: Ham, T. (1851). New diggings, Ballarat [picture] / T. Ham, Engraver; p. 23 (top): Victorian Parliamentary Library, (bottom): Gift of W Max Bell and Norman Belcher, 1923/Gift of W Max Bell and Norman Belcher, 1923. Photographer: Terence Bogue; p. 24: S Shang / 500px/500Px Plus/Getty Images; p. 25: Cotton, J. (1845). An encampment of Aboriginal Australians on the banks of the Yarra; p. 26: Sheila Terry/Science Photo Library; p. 27 (left): American & Australasian Photographic Company/Mitchell Library, State Library of New South Wales, (right): American & Australasian Photographic Company/Mitchell Library, State Library of New South Wales; p. 28: Grosse, Frederick & Chevalier, Nicholas. (186-]). Emigrants landing at the Queen's Wharf, Melbourne. Retrieved from http://nla.gov.au/nla.obj-135652434; p. 29: Damman, G. M. (1895). [Cobb & Co. coach and horses outside Harcourt, Warburton, Victoria; p. 30: Andris Torms/Dreamstime.com; back cover: Gill, S. T. (1872). Diggers on road to Bendigo / S.T.G.

ISBN 978 0 17 033470 9

Cengage Learning Australia
Level 5, 80 Dorcas Street
Southbank VIC 3006 Australia
Phone: 1300 790 853
Email: aust.nelsonprimary@cengage.com

For learning solutions, visit **cengage.com.au**

Printed in Malaysia by Papercraft
1 2 3 4 5 6 7 29 28 27 26 25

Nelson acknowledges the Traditional Owners and Custodians of the lands of all First Nations Peoples. We pay respect to Elders past and present, and extend that respect to all First Nations Peoples today.

Contents

Why People Seek Gold	**4**
What Is a Gold Rush?	**8**
Australian Gold Rushes	**10**
People on the Australian Goldfields	**14**
Men	**14**
Women and Children	**18**
First Nations Peoples	**22**
Chinese Miners	**26**
Immigrants from Other Places	**28**
Changed Forever	**30**
Glossary	**31**
Index	**32**

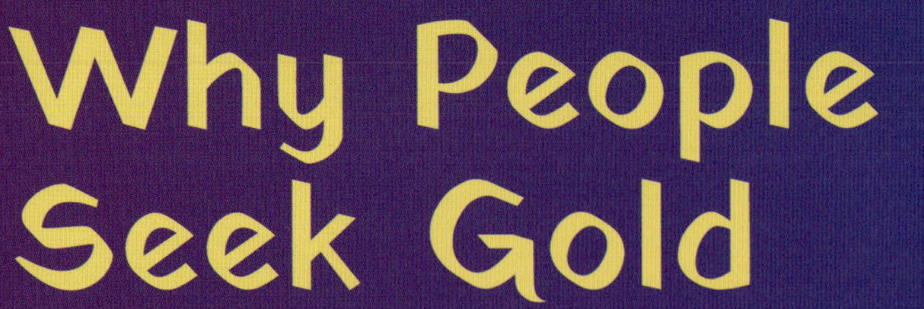

Why People Seek Gold

Of the more than 90 metals that have been discovered on Earth, none holds such a special place in our hearts as gold.

For thousands of years, humans have been fascinated by gold. Many ancient civilisations, including those of Egypt, China, Rome, Greece and the Maya, used gold as jewellery, for decoration and as **currency**.

an ancient Egyptian necklace

some ancient Roman coins

a piece of ancient Mayan jewellery

an ancient Chinese goblet

But what is it that causes "gold fever" – a feeling that can grab hold of the human mind and make people pack up their lives, kiss their loved ones goodbye and leave their homes in the hope of finding gold?

One answer is that gold is rare. The rarer something is, the more **valuable** it is, because fewer people can own it.

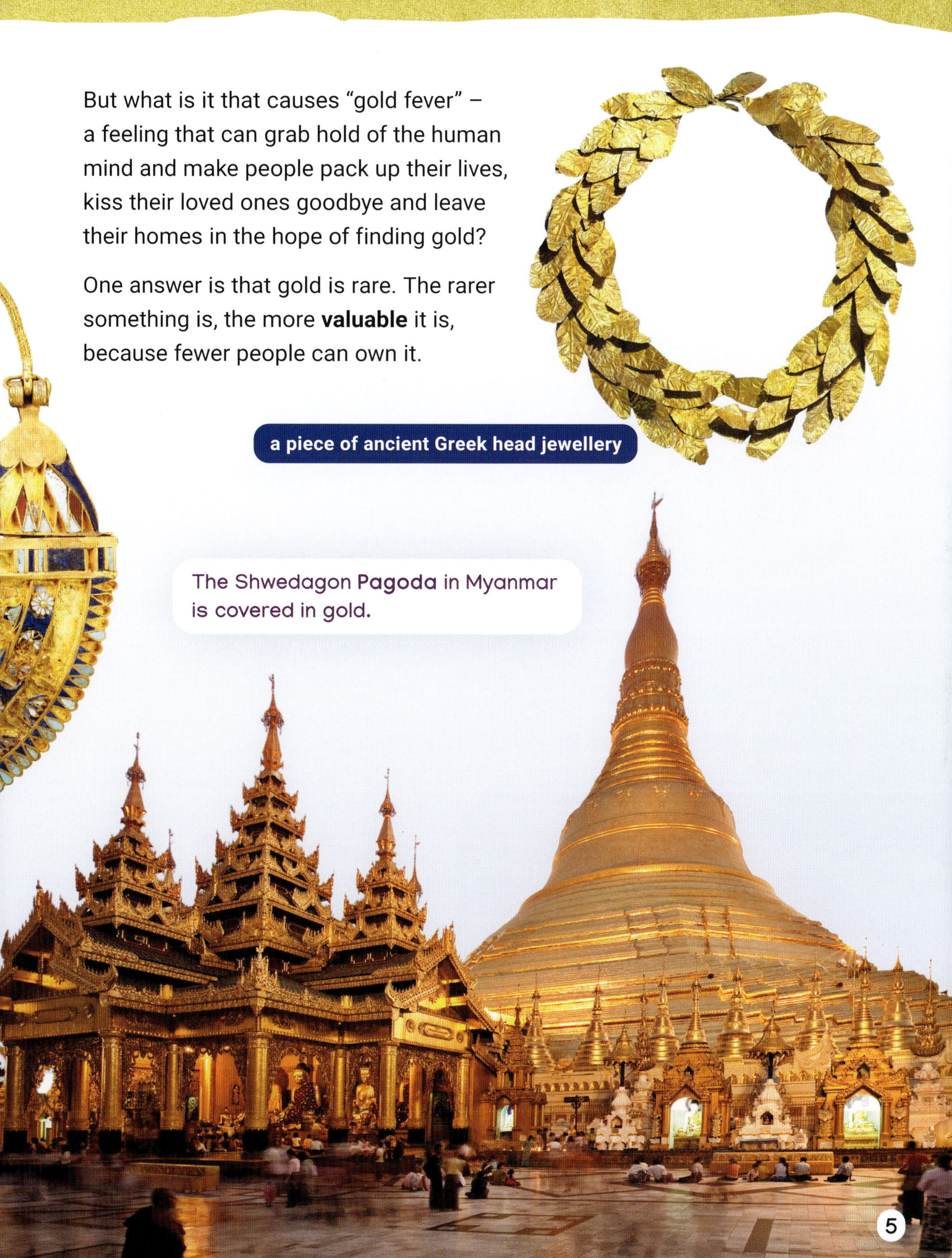

a piece of ancient Greek head jewellery

The Shwedagon **Pagoda** in Myanmar is covered in gold.

The process of digging up metals such as gold from the ground is known as mining. It has been estimated that only about 210 000 tonnes of gold have been mined throughout history. Roughly that much **iron ore** is mined around the world every 45 minutes!

Even huge modern gold mines do not produce a lot of gold.

Another appeal of gold is its bright yellow colour. It can shine. It can glitter. Many people consider it more beautiful to look at than most other metals.

Glittering gold jewellery is displayed in jewellery shop windows.

Solid Gold

If all the gold that has ever been found was melted into one cube, it would only measure about 22 metres on each side.

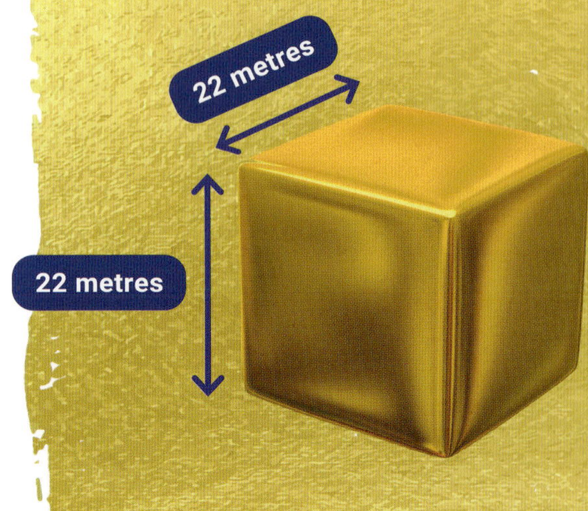

Gold is also very **malleable**. Many metals crack or split if they are hammered or pressed, but gold can be reshaped easily, for example, into round coins or jewellery such as rings.

Gold has lots of uses in industry, such as in electronics and in space technology.

These are just some of the reasons why humans have long been gold seekers and have dreamed of getting rich by finding gold.

some gold shaped into a ring

a computer chip made with gold

The James Webb Space Telescope has 18 gold mirrors.

What Is a Gold Rush?

A gold rush occurs when many people move to one area after gold has been discovered there. Gold rushes can change towns, cities, states and even whole countries. Small towns, or even areas where no one has lived before, can quickly be transformed into bustling cities during a gold rush. Suddenly the towns need more accommodation, food, equipment, police, entertainment, and many other **goods** and **services**.

Although digging for gold has been going on for thousands of years, it didn't cause people to travel long distances until the nineteenth century. Communication before then was much slower, which meant people didn't hear about gold discoveries so easily. Transportation was also much more limited before that time.

However, a way of communicating called the "telegram" was invented in the 1800s. A telegram was a message sent through special electrical wires and then printed out. This invention meant more people heard about gold discoveries faster.

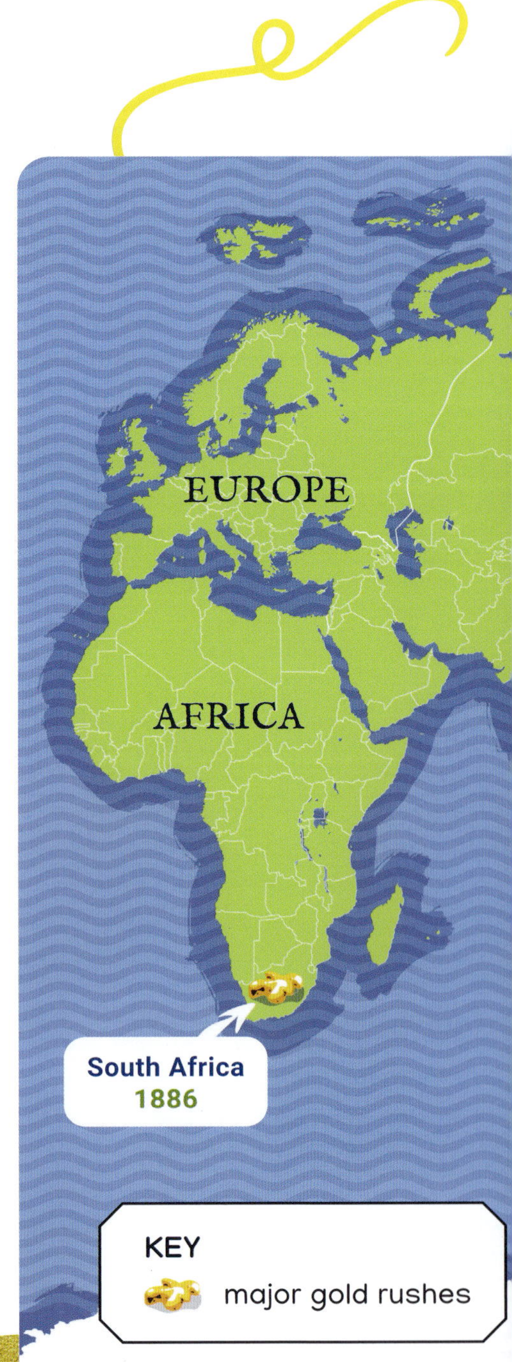

At the same time, there were developments in transport, such as the invention of trains and improvements in boat and ship building. These technological changes helped gold rushes occur across the world.

Some of the most famous gold rushes are those that happened in Brazil, the USA (particularly in California), Australia, Aotearoa New Zealand, Venezuela and South Africa.

Famous Gold Rushes Around the World

Australian Gold Rushes

In Australia, the first gold rush occurred in the middle of the nineteenth century. On 12 February 1851, four **prospectors** – Edward Hargraves, John Lister and brothers William and James Tom – found five specks of gold in Lewis Ponds Creek near Bathurst in New South Wales. They had been searching for gold because the **governor** of the New South Wales **colony**, Sir Charles Augustus FitzRoy, had offered a huge reward for anyone who discovered gold there. The governor knew that such a find would start a gold rush and bring people and wealth to the colony.

Keen for the reward money, Edward Hargraves raced to the governor in Sydney, and reported the find before the others could join him. The governor gave Hargraves the reward, as well as the promise of some extra money, to be paid to him over many years. Hargraves was also given a job in charge of some large areas of land. The other three prospectors, John Lister and the Tom brothers, didn't receive any reward or thanks.

Edward Hargreaves was pictured as a hero in this painting from June 1851.

A report in a newspaper from 17 May 1851 gives an idea of how quickly the town of Bathurst and its surrounding area became overrun with people as a result of the discovery of gold:

> The discovery of ... one immense goldfield, has produced a tremendous excitement in the town of Bathurst and the surrounding **districts** ... A complete ... madness appears to have seized almost every member of the community.
>
> *Bathurst Free Press*

This drawing from 1851 shows daily life in the goldfields in New South Wales.

On 6 July 1851, gold was discovered in Clunes, near Ballarat in Victoria, by prospector James Esmond. The search for gold in Ballarat started because the governor of Victoria, Charles La Trobe, had also offered a reward for its discovery – mainly to try to stop people leaving his colony for New South Wales.

Although tiny amounts of gold had been found before in Victoria, Esmond's discovery was the first to be sold in that state. It sparked a gold rush so big that in the 1850s, more than one-third of the world's gold was found in Victoria.

James Esmond, 1851

This painting from 1852 shows men looking for gold in a river bed at Mount Alexander.

The **population** of Australia almost tripled during the gold rushes of the 1850s as huge numbers of people moved to New South Wales and Victoria from other countries.

Further gold rushes occurred in Queensland in the 1860s and 1870s, and in Western Australia in the 1890s. Smaller gold rushes took place in Tasmania in the 1850s, South Australia in 1868 and in the Northern Territory in the 1870s.

Australian Gold Rushes

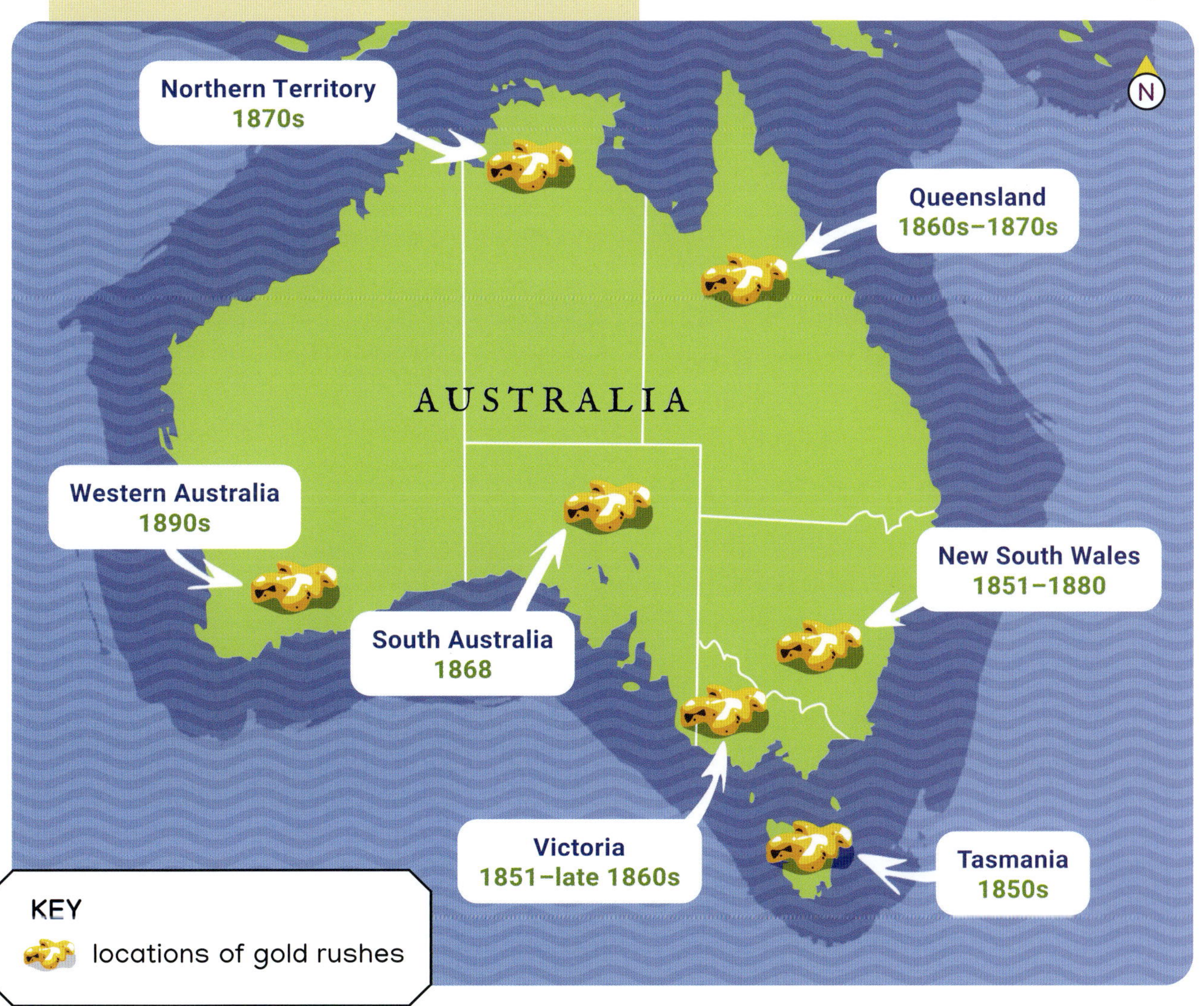

People on the Australian Goldfields

Many different types of people moved to the Australian goldfields. But who were these people? How did they live and work? And how did the gold rushes affect the **First Nations peoples** of those places?

Men

The first people who travelled to the goldfields were fit, married and unmarried men from cities such as Melbourne and Sydney. They were the first to hear about the gold discoveries and could get to the goldfields quickly in horse-drawn carriages or on foot. They were usually happy to leave their jobs because they didn't earn much, and the idea of finding gold was irresistible. Most of these men were Australian-born with a **British** or Irish background, or had moved to Australia from Britain or Ireland.

This painting shows men using a wooden "gold cradle" to find gold amongst rock and mud on the goldfields.

For most people on the goldfields, the best shelter was a tent.

At first, the gold seekers had few places to stay. Even as houses and hotels were built, the population on the goldfields continued to increase so rapidly that most of the men had to camp next to the rivers where they hoped to find gold. The lucky ones had tents in which they could sleep at night or shelter from the rain and heat. However, many couldn't afford tents and instead slept in the open, wrapping blankets and other materials around themselves to keep warm at night.

This painting of a miner's camp in Castlemaine, Victoria, shows how basic living conditions were.

Prospectors had two main ways of looking for gold: panning and mining. Gold panning required little money to get started, as the only equipment needed was a pan to **sift** dirt from the creeks and streams. Small pieces of gold could sometimes be found among the dirt. This type of gold, found on or just below the river bed, is known as "alluvial gold".

a gold pan

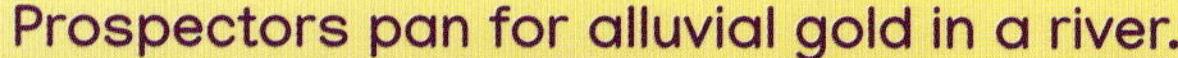

Prospectors pan for alluvial gold in a river.

Most gold nuggets were very small, but some miners found large ones.

Wealthier men, or groups of men who put all their money together, went gold mining. This required buying equipment and paying the government to mine a piece of land that nobody else was allowed on. The miners would dig underground, building mineshafts, which were passages that they could crawl through. Under the ground, miners could find larger pieces of gold than those found by people panning in the rivers.

Later, when mining companies were formed, some of the gold panners switched to working in the mines. They were paid a **wage**, rather than earning money from finding and selling their own gold.

This photo of a gold mine in Ballarat, Victoria, dates from about 1900.

The World's Largest Nugget

On 19 October 1871, a nugget weighing 285 kilograms was found in the Star of Hope gold mine in New South Wales. While it was described as the world's largest gold nugget, only about one-third of the nugget was actually gold. The rest was quartz and slate. But it still made the mine owners very wealthy.

Mine manager Bernhardt Otto Holtermann poses with the huge nugget.

Not many gold panners or miners got rich. Unfortunately, what they often did get was sick – as did everyone in the camps. Human waste and mining waste were dumped into the rivers, so the water became polluted. People used the river water for drinking and cleaning, so diseases spread throughout the camps.

Most of the food the miners ate had to be brought in from other places, which meant it was expensive and the quality was often poor. Living on the goldfields was no picnic!

Women and Children

Although most of the people who first moved to the goldfields were men, soon thousands of women and children were living there, too. Within three years of the start of the Victorian gold rush, more than one-third of the population of Ballarat, the largest gold fields town, was women and children.

Most of the women on the goldfields were immigrants who had moved to Australia with their husbands to seek their fortune. Australian women whose husbands left for the goldfields were more likely to stay in their home town, particularly if they had children. They didn't want to disrupt their children's lives.

Whole families lived in tents on the goldfields.

The luckiest women and children were those who lived in houses or hotels in the goldfields towns, but such accommodation wasn't cheap. Most women and children were squashed into tents with their husbands and fathers.

Children who were old enough would help their fathers pan for gold, or even dig underground. It was dirty, dangerous work. Some children drowned in the rivers or had other accidents. A few communities on the goldfields tried to set up schools in tents, but most children preferred, or were forced, to help find gold.

The children in this painting from 1885 are panning for gold.

Two children sit with adult miners at the top of a mine near Gulgong, New South Wales, in the 1870s.

Although most women on the goldfields worked raising children and running households, some searched for gold alongside their husbands. However, other men didn't always like having women working beside them. To avoid being bothered by them, some women dressed up as men.

Not all of the women on the goldfields were married. Some went to the goldfields to work as servants for wealthier families, or in shops, or even to do jobs that were usually done by men, such as being a **blacksmith** or a brick maker.

Three women pan for gold in a creek.

Jeanette Gribble owned this shop in the goldfields town of Gulgong in New South Wales.

With hundreds of thousands of people living and working in the goldfields and the towns near them, people had opportunities to make a lot of money. It wasn't just men who set up businesses and sold goods and services. Many women did so, too. For example, Catherine Bentley ran the Eureka Hotel in Ballarat. Other women grew and sold food; sewed and repaired clothes; and even set up theatre companies and other forms of entertainment for the miners.

COLONY OF VICTORIA.

£2 10s. £2 10s.

District in which issued

Date

QUARTERLY

BUSINESS LICENSE.

Issued to under the provisions of the Act of the Governor and Council, 18 Victoria, No. in force until

NOT TRANSFERABLE.

All business owners needed a licence like this one.

A Long Walk

Martha Clendinning was born in Ireland and migrated to Australia in 1853 with her sister, Sarah, and their husbands. After their husbands went to Ballarat to prospect for gold, Martha and Sarah decided to travel from Melbourne to Ballarat and open a store on the goldfields.

Martha found the horse and cart ride so bumpy that she got out of the cart and walked the whole way, earning the nickname, "the lady that walked to Ballarat".

First Nations Peoples

The land where gold was found around Australia was home to First Nations peoples. But this didn't stop Europeans and other non-First Nations people from moving in and using it as they wished. By the time of the gold rushes, settlements had been established on land belonging to First Nations peoples without their permission for decades. The arrival of more non-First Nations people during the gold rushes made this situation worse.

The gold rushes had a huge impact on many First Nations peoples. Their land suffered environmental damage through water pollution and the destruction of trees, which were cut down by miners and used for firewood and for building huts. First Nations people suffered from diseases brought in by the Europeans and other immigrants. Many also had their lives and health affected by the alcohol that was common in camps.

This 1851 artwork of Ballarat shows First Nations people next to a fire in the foreground.

First Nations people didn't sit back and simply watch the miners, though. They participated in the gold rushes in several ways.

First Nations police on horseback take a prisoner from the goldfields at Ballarat to Melbourne.

Some First Nations people worked as guides for miners who wanted to explore areas untouched by mining in the hope of finding a new goldfield. Other First Nations people worked for the police, helping to maintain security, collecting taxes, and escorting gold from the goldfields to capital cities such as Melbourne.

To First Nations people of the time, gold was of little value. It didn't have a practical use. However, many saw the **economic** benefits of the gold rush, and sold food, clothes, rugs and other goods to the miners.

This painting shows two miners bargaining with a First Nations family for a possum-skin cloak.

Some First Nations people became gold seekers themselves, recognising the "fever" that gold caused in the rest of the population. A reporter writing in the *Maryborough Advertiser* newspaper on 1 October 1866 recounted this story.

> On Saturday morning, a party of [First Nations people] commenced a search for gold on the pipeclay at the White Hills ... and in a very short time they discovered pieces which they sold for 12 shillings, 15 shillings, and 10 pounds odd. They say the same party were successful some time since in the neighbourhood of Amherst and Talbot.
>
> *Maryborough Advertiser*

Before the gold rush, First Nations people lived on land rich with forests and clean rivers.

The gold rushes provided some First Nations people employment and the opportunity to gain wealth. However, they also resulted in the loss and destruction of land, and the spread of alcohol and diseases within First Nations communities.

Stolen Land!

In Victoria, the main groups of people whose land was taken away from them during the gold rush were the Wathaurong and Djadjawurrung people.

This painting shows a First Nations woman in her camp near the Yarra River in Victoria.

Chinese Miners

Some Chinese people were already living in Australia before the gold rushes of the 1850s. But it was gold that encouraged tens of thousands of Chinese people to leave their homes and sail to the Australian goldfields to make their fortunes. Most Chinese immigrants came from southern China, where poverty, war and China's closeness to Australia made relocating an easy choice. By the end of the 1850s, about 40 000 Chinese people were living in Australia, mostly on and around the goldfields.

This artwork shows two Chinese miners using a gold cradle to look for gold on the Australian goldfields.

The Chinese language and traditions were very different from those of the prospectors from European backgrounds. Many European miners reacted to these differences with **racism** towards the Chinese miners, and sometimes with violence. For example, in 1857, at Buckland River, Victoria, a group of European men killed four Chinese miners, burnt all their tents and shops, and stole their gold. They saw the presence of Chinese miners as a threat to their own chances of finding the gold that remained.

Some of this racism even came from the government. The Victorian government passed a law that limited the number of Chinese immigrants who could arrive in Victoria by boat. Instead, Chinese people went to other colonies first, particularly South Australia, and then walked or travelled on horseback to the goldfields in Victoria.

A man stands in front of a Chinese boarding house in Gulgong, New South Wales.

Chinese businessman On Gay owned a shop in the goldfields town of Hill End, New South Wales.

Despite the racism and violence they faced, many Chinese people stayed and settled permanently in Australia after the gold rushes. They opened shops, restaurants and other businesses, and became an important part of Australian society.

Immigrants from Other Places

Before the discovery of gold, fewer than half a million people were living in the various colonies in Australia. Within ten years, that number had almost tripled.

People flocked from all over the world to try to make their fortune. Most of them came from Britain and Ireland. During the gold rushes, about 300 000 people came from England and Wales, 100 000 from Scotland and more than 80 000 from Ireland. Immigrants also arrived from Aotearoa New Zealand and other South Pacific islands, Germany and North America. The number of immigrants was almost the same number of people as the entire population of Australia when the gold rushes started.

Unlike the Chinese immigrants, most British immigrants did not suffer from racism or abuse. After all, about three-quarters of the Australian population at the time had a British background. That doesn't mean there weren't problems. The Irish were fiercely anti-British, and were themselves the target of anti-Irish discrimination.

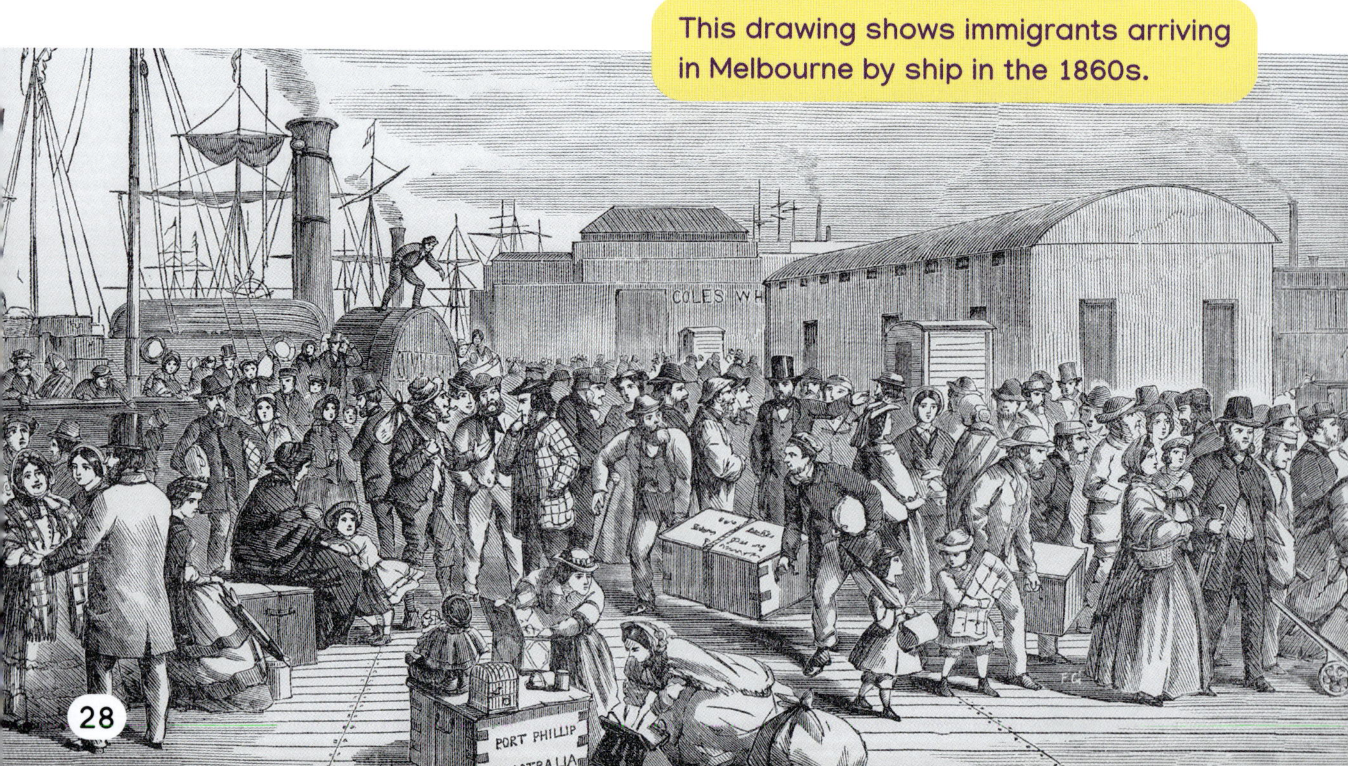

This drawing shows immigrants arriving in Melbourne by ship in the 1860s.

In the USA, the California gold rush of the late 1840s had attracted prospectors from all over the world, including Australia. The discovery of gold in Australia not only brought many Australians home from California, but Americans and people from other countries who hadn't "struck it lucky" in the USA came with them.

Cobb & Co

One of the Americans who settled in Melbourne was Freeman Cobb, who started the successful Cobb & Co coach business.

Cobb's coaches were carriages pulled by horses. They transported people and goods between Melbourne and the Victorian goldfields.

Passengers crowd inside and on the roof of a Cobb & Co coach in the late 1860s.

The Australian gold rush also attracted significant numbers of immigrants from Italy, Greece, Cyprus and Croatia. The gold rush was the start of Australia becoming a **multicultural** society.

Changed Forever

The gold rushes of the 1850s changed Australia forever. They dramatically increased the population, attracting immigrants from all over the world, and at one stage made Melbourne one of the most **prosperous** cities on the planet.

The landscape of Australia was changed, too, as new towns appeared while some old towns lost their populations, never to recover.

The goldfields were home to many different people, including thousands of women and children, and people from a range of backgrounds.

The gold rushes also had a major impact on the lives of the First Nations peoples on whose lands the gold mining and panning took place.

All these people had different experiences and stories, and their lives were forever changed. All because of a shiny metal ... gold!

Some modern towns and cities like Ballarat in Victoria may never have existed without the gold rushes.

Glossary

blacksmith (*noun*)	a person who makes horseshoes and tools from metal
British (*adjective*)	from the island of Britain (including England, Scotland and Wales) or Northern Ireland
colony (*noun*)	a country or area under the control of a more powerful country that is often far away
currency (*noun*)	a system of using objects such as coins to buy goods and services
districts (*noun*)	areas of land
economic (*adjective*)	to do with making money
First Nations peoples (*noun*)	the first peoples living in an area
goods (*noun*)	items that are bought and sold
governor (*noun*)	the official head of a colony or state
iron ore (*noun*)	a mineral found in rocks that is used to make steel
malleable (*adjective*)	able to be hammered or pressed into a different shape
multicultural (*adjective*)	made up of people from many different cultural backgrounds
Pagoda (*noun*)	a temple
population (*noun*)	all the people who live in a place
prospectors (*noun*)	people looking for valuable minerals and metals
prosperous (*adjective*)	wealthy and successful
racism (*noun*)	unfair treatment of people because of their race
services (*noun*)	tasks that are done for a customer
sift (*verb*)	to sort through something
valuable (*adjective*)	worth a lot of money
wage (*noun*)	money paid to someone for doing a job

Index

accommodation 8, 15, 19
Ballarat 12, 17, 18, 21, 22, 23, 30
Bathurst 10, 11
Bentley, Catherine 21
British immigrants 14, 28, 31
children 18–19, 20, 30
Chinese immigrants 26–27, 28
Clendinning, Martha 21
communication 8
entertainment 8, 21
Esmond, James 12
First Nations peoples 14, 22–25, 30, 31
food 8, 17, 21, 23
gold nuggets 16, 17
Hargraves, Edward 10
Irish immigrants 14, 28
iron ore 6, 31
Lister, John 10
mining 6, 16–17, 19, 23, 30
panning 16, 19, 20, 30
pollution 17, 22
population 13, 15, 18, 28–29, 30, 31
prospectors 10, 12, 16, 27, 29, 31
racism 27, 28, 31
telegram 8
Tom, William and James 10
transport 8, 9, 14, 21, 27, 29
women 18–21, 30